Stefen Bernath

HERBS
Coloring Book

Dover Publications, Inc., New York

Publisher's Note

Long before the time of Theophrastus (*ca.* 370–287 B.C.) and Hippocrates (*ca.* 460–377 B.C.) herbs were being grown for their culinary and medicinal value. The monasteries of the Middle Ages were never without their herb gardens, and the great Elizabethan herbals contained fascinating lore about the uses of thyme, savory, rosemary, and basil. In recent years there has been a revival of interest in these unusual plants that provide fragrance, flavoring, medicine, and nourishment.

Stefen Bernath, author of Dover's *Garden Flowers Coloring Book* and *House Plants Coloring Book*, now turns to herbs for this new collection. The plates are arranged alphabetically by common name, and authoritative scientific names are given. All the herbs are shown in full color on the covers of this volume. In addition you might want to seek out the herbs themselves in gardens or flower shops, or even grow your own herbs at home. In any case you will have the fun of coloring the herbs and also getting acquainted with these ancient plants that today are living legends.

Published in Canada by General Publishing Company, Ltd.,
30 Lesmill Road. Don Mills, Toronto, Ontario.
Published in the United Kingdom by Constable and
Company, Ltd., 10 Orange Street, London WC2H 7EG.

Herbs Coloring Book is a new work, first published by
Dover Publications, Inc., in 1977.

DOVER *Pictorial Archive* SERIES

International Standard Book Number: 0-486-23499-1

Manufactured in the United States of America
Dover Publications, Inc.
180 Varick Street
New York, N.Y. 10014

1. Angelica (*Angelica archangelica*)

2. Anise (*Pimpinella anisum*)

3. Basil (*Ocymum basilicum*)

4. Bay leaves (Sweet bay, Bay laurel, *Laurus nobilis*)

5. Borage (*Borago officinalis*)

6. Calendula (Pot marigold, *Calendula officinalis*)

7. Caraway (*Carum carvi*)

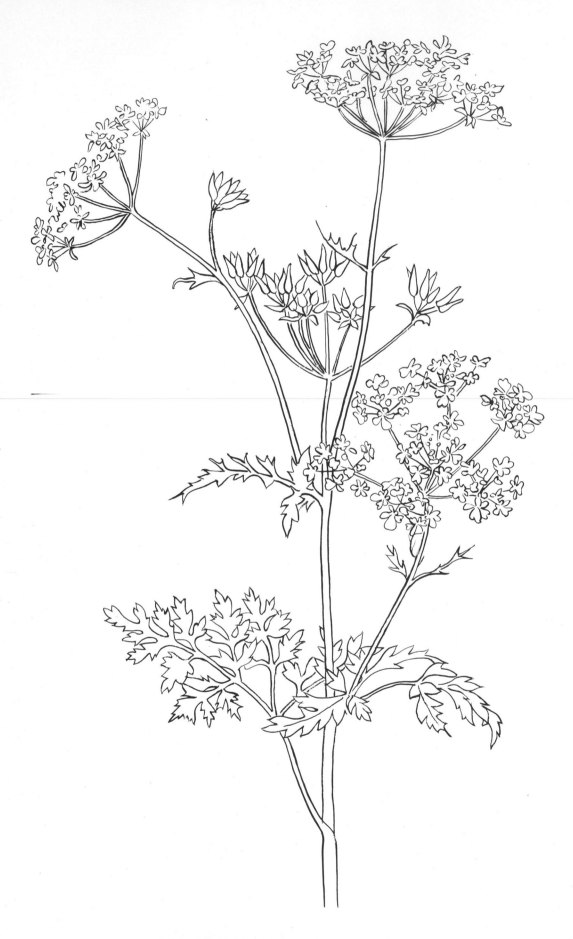

8. Chervil (*Anthriscus cerefolium*)

9. Chives (*Allium schoenoprasum*)

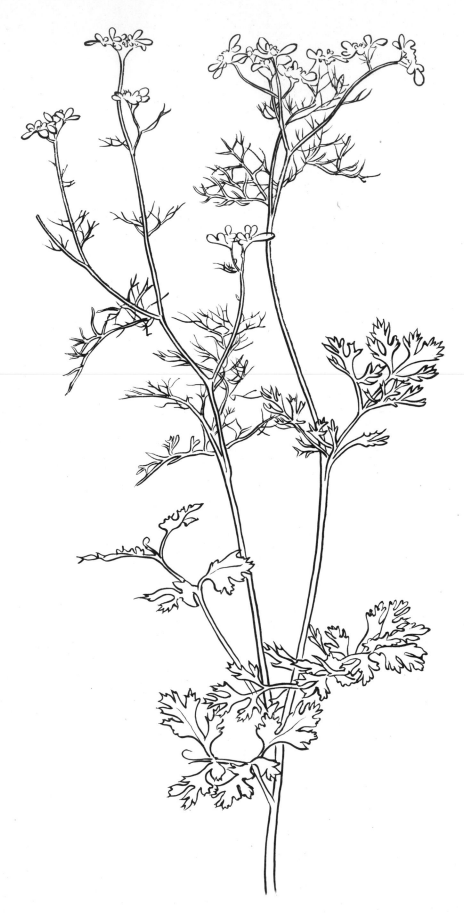

10. Coriander (*Coriandrum sativum*)

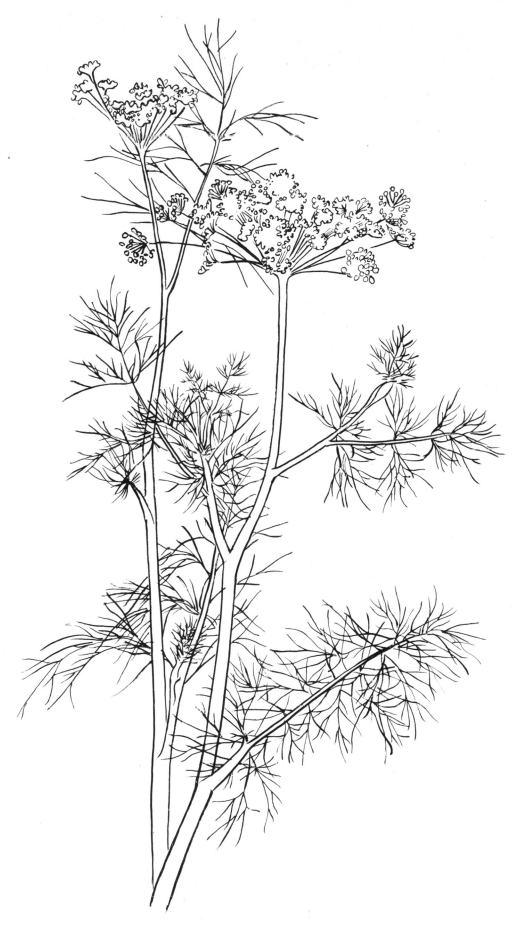

11. Dill (*Anethum graveolens*)

12. Fennel (*Foeniculum dulce*)

13. Horehound (*Marrubium vulgare*)

14. Lavender (*Lavandula vera*)

15. Lemon thyme (*Thymus serpyllum*)

16. Lemon verbena (*Lippia citriodora*)

17. Mallow (*Malva rotundifolia*)

18. Marjoram (*Origanum marjorana*)

19. Oregano (*Origanum vulgare*)

20. Parsley (*Carum petroselinum*)

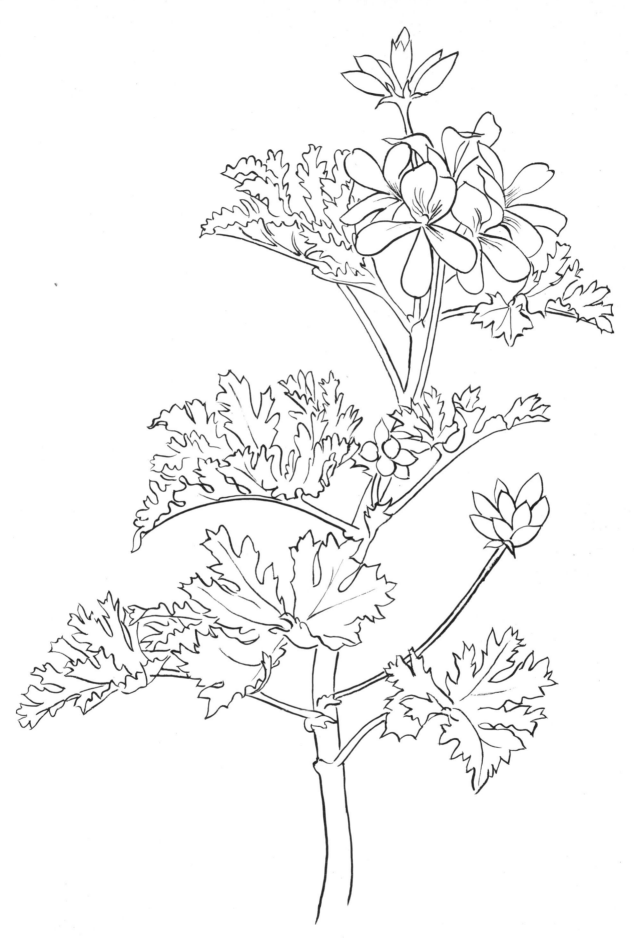

21. Rose geranium (*Pelargonium roseum*)

22. Rosemary (*Rosmarinus officinalis*)

23. Saffron (*Crocus sativus*)

24. Sage (*Salvia officinalis*)

25. Spearmint, Peppermint (*Mentha spicata, Mentha piperita*)

26. Summer Savory (*Satureia hortensis*)

27. Tansy (*Tanacetum vulgare*)

28. Tarragon (*Artemisia dracunculus*)

29. Thyme (*Thymus vulgaris*)

30. Woodruff (*Asperula odorata*)